Witch Hazel and the Monkey

E. Larreula   R. Capdevila   A. Wilkinson

Cambridge University Press

Cambridge   New York   New Rochelle   Melbourne   Sydney

Now we witches are not just anybody. Our favourite time of the day is the dark, dark night. I remember one terrible summer. The days were so hot and so long that my owl, Goggletoot, and I got fed up waiting for the cool night to come.

We had nothing left to eat but an old bone, one
fly, a few frogs, five old lizard eggs and some
hard rolls. But it was too hot for us to go
hunting for food in the daylight, and by night-
time there was nothing left for us. 'Poor Witch
Hazel!' sighed Goggletoot. 'We need someone
to help us,' I said.

The next morning as I was taking out my curlers, I had an idea! 'Goggletoot! Let's go to Africa and get a monkey! Monkeys like looking for food, and they love hot weather too.'

We were soon packed and ready
for the long journey to Africa. I
fetched my blue zoom-broom from
the garage.

It was my best broom for flying long distances, but I decided to take it to Ted at his old car yard so he could have a look over it.

He gave me a wing mirror so I could see what was coming up from behind. Goggletoot was cross because he could not sit at his usual place at the front. 'It doesn't look a bit like a wing to me,' he said grumpily.

We zoomed over land and sea, and reached Africa in no time. But the sun grew hotter and hotter as we flew over the great Sahara desert. Poor Goggletoot felt so ill he thought he might slip off my back and land on one of the camels or get buried deep in the soft sand.

My dear old zoom-broom had done a good job
getting us all the way to Africa. But when we
reached the jungle, I think the hot sun started to
frizzle its magic bristles. Suddenly it flew head-
over-heels and dived into the jungle below.

After our crash-landing,
we felt hot and a little
dizzy. So we sat down
under a tree to have some
lunch. Goggletoot asked if
he could have one of my
frog rolls, because the
worms in the jungle looked
a bit of a mouthful.

We felt a lot stronger after eating our lunch, so we set about catching a monkey for us to take home. I took a bag of monkey-nuts from my travel basket and scattered them on the ground to bring the monkeys down from the trees. 'Monkey, monkey, monkey!'

But, before I could grab a tail, they had scampered down the tree, snatched the monkey-nuts and scampered up the tree again.

It was time for one of my clever ideas. I took a little longer than usual to think up this one because the heat was so bad. I tied Goggletoot to a tree and left a large ball of rope beside him.

Now I had heard that monkeys like to copy everything we do. And my idea was that the monkeys would start tying each other to the trees. Then it would be easy to catch one.

I pretended to read my newspaper while I
watched them out of the corner of my eye.
I was pleased when they took the rope and
started to wind it . . . not round themselves
but . . . oh dear . . .

. . . round me, and tied me very
tightly to a tree!

The little rascals climbed up the trees again to read my newspaper! Now, even the cleverest ideas can go wrong. You will remember that a witch is not at her best in the daylight.

But it was not too long before night fell. As it grew cooler and darker, I felt my magic getting stronger again. I remembered a spell my mother, Witch Camomile had taught me.

'Don't worry Goggletoot,' I whispered. 'We'll be out of these ropes any moment . . .
Grow you thin, Grow you thin
Into merest bones and skin!'
And, quick as a flash, I grew thin and the ropes fell loose round my feet.

I quickly untied Goggletoot, and we raced off
after the nearest monkey. Suddenly, Goggletoot
screeched,'A rhinoceros is chasing us, he's after
the monkey nuts . . . EEEK!'

At that moment I caught a monkey
by the tail and tied him to my
zoom-broom.

We jumped behind the next tree and I just had
time to shout,
 '*Big you were, oh rhino spiny,
 Now you are a rhino tiny!*'
And in a twinkle of magic he was as small as a dog!

But now he was small he was much nippier, and he raced round the tree to get another monkey-nut. I was so surprised that I fell over backwards and landed on his little horn.
'OW . . . OUCH!'

I squawked so loudly that all the monkeys swung down from the trees to have a look. The rascals started to copy me. They jumped around screeching, holding their hands on their bottoms. I felt terrible!

I was so relieved when at last we set off home
with the monkey. My bottom was so sore I
could not sit down once on the journey home.
And Goggletoot was quite exhausted too. Only
the monkey looked quite well. 'Those are
funny looking trees!' he piped.

Once we were home I went to bed for a week. Our monkey Affi was very good to us. He put hot water-bottles on my sore bottom and ice-packs on Goggletoot's hot, aching head. We were pleased to have someone so helpful at home with us. And we soon cheered up because Affi was always smiling and doing funny tricks. By the way, we called him Affi because we had to go all the way to Africa to find him – worst luck!

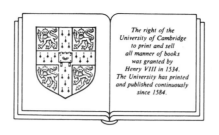

Published by the Press Syndicate of the University of Cambridge
The Pitt Building, Trumpington Street, Cambridge CB2 1RP
32 East 57th Street, New York, NY 10022, USA
10 Stamford Road, Oakleigh, Melbourne 3166, Australia

Originally published in Spanish 1986 as *La Bruja Aburidda y La mona*
by Editorial Ariel S.A., Barcelona
© 1986 Editorial Ariel S.A.
First published in English by Cambridge University Press 1988 as *Witch Hazel
and the Monkey*. English edition © Cambridge University Press 1988

Printed in Spain

British Library Cataloguing in Publication Data
Larreula, E.
Witch hazel and the monkey.
I. Title II. Capdevila, R. III. Wilkinson, A.
IV. La Bruja Aburrida y la mona. *English*
863′.64[J] PZ7

ISBN 0 521 35341 6

If you have enjoyed this book you might enjoy *A Witch called Hazel.*

GE

Depósito Legal B. 42399/1987 - SORPAMA, S. A.